What kind of cigarettes do Jewish mothers smoke?
(See page 9)

What did the WASP mother ask her daughter when she learned she'd had an affair?
(See page 14)

How does a Greek firing squad line up?
(See page 35)

Why do men have more brains than dogs?
(See page 71)

What can a duck do that a goose can't and a lawyer should?
(See page 85)

What do Madonna and a Boeing 747 have in common?
(See page 97)

Also by Blanche Knott
Published by St. Martin's Press

Blanche Knott's

Truly Tasteless Jokes XII

ST. MARTIN'S PAPERBACKS

TRULY TASTELESS JOKES XII

ISBN: 0-312-92973-0

Printed in the United States of America

St. Martin's Paperbacks edition/November 1992

10 9 8 7 6 5 4 3 2 1

to Rick and Mena

TABLE OF CONTENTS

POLISH

The Polish guy was thrilled to get a jigsaw puzzle for his birthday. He set all sixteen pieces out on a card table and every day when he got home from the office he'd set to work on it. Finally, one day he jumped up from the table and ran to the phone. "Sylvia!" he cried, "remember the puzzle you gave me? I finished it!"

"Gee, Stan, that's great," responded his friend after a little hesitation. "But you mean to say it took you three months to put it together?"

"Not bad, eh?" Stan said proudly. "On the box it says, 'Two to five years.'"

●

The three Poles went on vacation together, and to save money they shared the same hotel room. But three big guys in a double bed didn't make for very comfortable sleeping quarters, so Nowicki gave up and moved onto the rug.

1

He was just about asleep when his buddy shook him by the shoulder. "You might as well get back in bed, Tommy—there's lots of room now."

•

How did the DA figure out there was a Polish mafia?

They found two Poles in an alley in Chicago; their heads were tied together, and they were shot in the hands.

•

Walenski had joined the Army Airborne with dreams of parachuting, but now that the moment had come for his first jump, he was pretty scared. The instructor assured him that all he had to do was count to ten and pull the cord. "Relax—even if your chute malfunctions, the reserve will open automatically. And our truck will be waiting for you at the drop site." With those comforting words, the instructor gave Walenski a shove, and he found himself plummeting towards the earth.

After a few seconds of pure terror, the private began counting, and pulled the ripcord right on time. Nothing happened. Trying to stay calm, Walenski waited for the reserve chute to open. Nothing happened. "Shit," he muttered as the ground rushed towards him, "I'll just bet the truck isn't there either."

•

Heard about the Polish library?

It has only one book—they haven't finished coloring the other one yet.

●

Why does the Second Polish Navy sail in glass-bottomed boats?

So they can keep an eye on the First Polish Navy.

●

Zabiski saved up his money for an excursion to Reno, where he soon found himself at the bar next to a very attractive brunette. "Say, could I buy you a drink?" he asked boldly.

"Forget it, buddy," she replied, not unkindly. "I'm gay."

Zabiski looked blank.

"I'm a lesbian," she elaborated.

Zabiski shook his head. "What's a lesbian?"

"See that woman over there?" She pointed at a lovely blonde waitress serving drinks on the far side of the room.

Zabiski nodded, perking up.

"Well, I'd like to take her up to my room," the brunette elaborated, "take all her clothes off, and nibble her tits and lick every curve and suck every inch of that sweet young thing, all night long."

At this, Zabiski burst into tears and buried his head in his arms.

"Why the hell're you crying?" asked his companion gruffly.

"I think I'm a lesbian, too," he sobbed.

•

Why are people all over Poland saving bowling balls?

They're making a rosary for Stachu of Liberty.

•

"We need to work out our defense," explained the lawyer appointed by the court after introducing himself to his client. "Now tell me, Mr. Kosinski—why was it you parked in that particular spot?"

The fellow scratched his head and explained, "Because the sign said 'Fine for Parking.' "

•

"I think the new medic's a crackpot," confessed Stokowski to Meyrowitz. "I went to see him about my piles, and he told me to drink carrot juice after a hot bath."

4

"You never know," commented Meyrowitz. "How'd the carrot juice taste?"

"Don't know yet; I've only drunk half the bath so far."

•

The two Polish machinists got a little time off and were taking a walk on the beach when a seagull unloaded on the first man's shoulder.

"Too bad," his buddy commiserated. "You want me to get some toilet paper?"

"Nah," he replied with a shrug. "It's probably a mile away by now."

•

When Krichevsky won the lottery everyone agreed that it couldn't have happened to a nicer guy. And indeed the first thing the big winner announced that he was going to do with the money was build three swimming pools for his friends to use.

"Why three?" asked the *Daily News* reporter.

"One with cold water that'll be really refreshing, one heated to eighty degrees for folks that like the water warm, and one empty."

"Empty?" pursued the reporter.

"Sure," explained Krichevsky. "Some of my friends can't swim."

5

How can you tell when a helicopter's been built for the Polish Army?

The pilot's chair is an ejection seat.

●

Two Polish girls saved up their money for a week's vacation in Maui. When they reached the hotel, they jumped into their bathing suits and headed for the beach. And no sooner had they waded into the surf than Wanda yelped, "A crab bit one of my toes!"

"Which one?" asked her companion, scurrying back up onto the beach after her.

"How should I know?" Wanda snapped. "All crabs look alike."

●

Did you hear what happened when, after years of debate, Poland finally sent four thousand soldiers to the Gulf?

Mexico didn't know what to do with 'em.

●

"Anything wrong, sir?" asked the cop of the man who was jumping up and down on the street corner as he waited for the light to change.

"Oh, no thanks, officer," answered Mielowski. "I just took my medicine, and I forgot to shake the bottle."

●

What's one idea that never got off the ground?
   The Polish Air Force.

●

"Now with that entree, either a white wine or a light red would be appropriate," the waiter graciously pointed out. "What may I serve you?"

"Suit yourself," replied the Polish diner cheerfully. "I'm color-blind."

●

"Daddy, here's a note from the teacher," said the little boy when he got home from school. "I'll read it to you: 'Dear Mr. Rubiak: Stash really ought to have the use of an encyclopedia.' Well, Dad, what about it?"

Without lifting his head from the racing form, Rubiak

grunted, "I walked to school when I was a kid, and so can you."

●

What did they find when they took down the Berlin Wall?

The Hide & Seek Champion of Poland.

JEWISH

What kind of cigarettes do Jewish mothers smoke?
  Gefiltered.

•

Rubin and Katz, two judges, were each arrested on speeding charges. When they arrived in court on the appointed day, no one else was there, so instead of wasting time waiting around, they decided to try each other. Motioning Rubin to the stand, Katz asked, "How do you plead?"

"Guilty."

"That'll be fifty dollars and a warning from the court." Katz stepped down, and the two judges shook hands and changed places.

"How do you plead?" asked Rubin.

"Guilty."

Katz reflected for a moment or two. "These speeding incidents are becoming all too common of late," he pointed out sternly. "In fact, this is the second such case in the last quarter of an hour. That'll be one hundred dollars and thirty days in jail."

•

For his fortieth birthday the nice Jewish boy received the usual two ties from his mother, this time a paisley and a solid. When he picked her up for dinner that night wearing the solid, old Mrs. Cohen took one look and snapped, "And what's wrong with the paisley?"

•

Why do Jewish mothers make great parole officers?
  They never let anyone finish a sentence.

•

Young Joel was overcome with desire for a young woman he'd just met. Rachel, however, made quite clear her intention of obeying her mother's instructions to marry a doctor.
  "Oh, my whole family follows the medical profession closely," offered Joel. "They're lawyers."

•

What's a genius?
   An average student with a Jewish mother.

•

A man was walking down a street in Belfast late one
night when a shadowy figure, face obscured by a ski
mask, stepped out in front of him. "Halt!" the figure
called out, blocking his path with an automatic rifle.
"Are you Catholic or Protestant?"
   The passerby wiped the sweat off his brow. "Neither,"
he replied with a sigh of relief. "I'm Jewish."
   The gunman pulled the trigger and blasted his victim
to smithereens. Turning away with a grin, he remarked,
"I must be the luckiest Arab in Ireland tonight."

•

What's the difference between a JAP and a pit bull?
   The jewelry.

•

What's a Jewish Nativity scene?
   Seven lawyers surrounding a car crash.

•

The two old ladies were enjoying their after-dinner coffee at the Catskills resort when a flasher darted over to their table and opened his coat.

"Hmmphhh," snorted Sadie without blinking an eye. "You call *that* a lining?"

•

What's the disease most commonly transmitted by Jewish mothers?

Guilt.

•

After the physical exam, the doctor summoned Fred into his office. "I hate to be the one to break it to you," he said, "but I'm afraid you've got cancer. An advanced case, too—you've only got six months to live."

"Oh my God," gasped Fred, turning white. When the news had sunk in he said, "Listen, Doc, do you have any suggestions as to how I could make the most of my remaining months?"

"Have you ever married?" asked the doctor.

"No."

"You might consider it," proposed the doctor. "After all, you'll need someone to look after you."

"Good point, Doc," mused Fred.

"May I make one more suggestion?" asked the doctor. When Fred nodded, he added, "Marry a nice Jewish girl."

"How come?" wondered Fred.

"It'll seem longer."

WASP

What did the WASP mother ask her daughter when she learned she'd had an affair?
   "Who catered it?"

•

What's the definition of a WASP?
   Someone who thinks Taco Bell is the Mexican phone company.

•

What did the WASP say when he totaled his car?
   "Well, that's the way the Mercedes Benz."

•

What's safe sex for preppies?
  Foreplay.

•

How come Stratford couldn't finish the corned beef sandwich he ordered at the country club?
  The chef ran out of raisin bread.

•

"Marry me, Blair, please marry me," begged Drew, down on his knees yet again. "If you don't I'll . . . I'll . . . I'll blow my brains out!"
  "Would you really, sweetie?" Blair giggled happily. "You'd really get the last laugh on Daddy—he tells everyone you don't have any."

•

What are two preppies making love?
  Competition.

•

The rector of St. Luke's Episcopal Church was a terribly proper young bachelor who became a terribly proper middle-aged bachelor, so the whole congregation was surprised when he finally announced his plans to marry

Miss Martingale, a woman active in many church programs. In due course the wedding occurred and the couple went off on their honeymoon, which was of course the subject of much entertaining speculation on the part of the congregation.

So on the rector's return, one of the acolytes screwed up his nerve and inquired, "How did you find it, Reverend?"

"With difficulty," answered the rector after reflecting briefly. Then he added softly, "Who would have thought to look under all that hair?"

•

Which figure among WASP women is lower, their IQs or their golf scores?

Neither. Their weight.

•

Graffito: WASPS MAKE THEIR MONEY THE OLD-FASHIONED WAY: THEY INHERIT IT!

•

What's the difference between a WASP wedding and a WASP funeral?

One less drunk.

The Sweetbriar sophomore spent an extremely daring spring vacation making the rounds of the New York art scene, most of it in the company of a trendy painter named Stuart. And when school was out, she took her parents to Stuart's gala opening.

The walls of the gallery were covered with huge nudes, and Binky's mother lost no time in ascertaining their distinct resemblance to her daughter. Grasping the girl firmly by the elbow and steering her into a quiet corner, she hissed, "Binky, these paintings look just like you. Don't tell me you could have done anything so tacky as to have posed in the nude."

"Of course not, Mummy," protested the girl, blushing deeply. "Stuart must have painted them from memory!"

•

How can you tell a preppie bitch?
She thinks she's too good to go fuck herself.

•

What do WASPs think Zimbabwe Rhodesia is?
A linebacker for the New England Patriots.

AFRICAN-AMERICAN

What's so special about Nelson Mandela?

He's the only black man who can stop New York traffic without Windex and a squeegie.

•

Two residents of a little town in Alabama, one white and one black, went downtown to register to vote in the upcoming election. The official in charge took down their names and addresses, then held up a bar of soap. "What's this?" he asked the white guy.

"A bar of soap."

"Right. You're registered." Then he turned to the black man and asked, "How many bubbles in this bar of soap?"

•

Did you hear about the rural Alabama high school's production of Snow White and the Seven Dwarfs?

They had to bus in Snow White.

•

"Hey, Jamal, how's it goin'?" Jawan beckoned his friend over to his side of the street.

"N-n-not so g-g-good," replied his friend, obviously pissed off. "I just ap-ap-ap-applied for a job as a r-r-r-radio announcer."

"No luck, huh?"

Jamal shook his head angrily. "Th-th-th-they won't hire bl-bl-blacks."

•

The elderly woman from a small Louisiana town walked into the bus station. "Gimme a ticket," she demanded of the man at the window.

"Certainly, ma'am—where to?" asked the agent. "What's your destination?"

"White folks always too damn curious about black folks' affairs. It ain't none of your business," she snapped. "Just gimme that ticket!"

•

When Brenda won big in the lottery, she lost no time in getting herself over to the fanciest fur store in town, where she finally settled on a full-length silver fox. As she stood there in front of the mirror a frown crossed Brenda's face, and she turned to the saleswoman. "Tell me the truth," she demanded. "Do you think this coat makes me look too Jewish?"

•

"Mrs. Atkinson, I have some news for you," declared Laverne when she arrived at her employer's house on Monday morning. "My divorce papers finally came through. I'm leaving that shiftless skunk for good and goin' back home to live with my folks."

Mrs. Atkinson blanched. "Oh my, Laverne. What am I going to do? Who's going to keep house for me?"

"Don't you worry," replied Laverne drily. "That no-count son of a bitch'll find a new wife in no time."

•

A very serious and dedicated young man, Jerome was a divinity student at the height of the freedom movement in the '60s. Each night he would pray for a divine sign of his destiny. And sure enough, one night he was answered by a deep voice booming down from Heaven. "Go to Mississippi, Jerome. Go to Mississippi!" the voice commanded.

"Okay Lord, I hear you," quavered the young fellow, terrified at the prospect. "All by myself?"

"Don't worry," said the voice reassuringly. "I'll be with you . . . as far as Memphis."

•

Why does football have so many black fans?

It's the only time a black man can chase a white one and 75,000 people will stand up and cheer.

•

When the Jacksons made the move out to the suburbs, their eight-year-old son Carl Jr. lost no time in making the acquaintance of the Jewish kid who lived next door. "We're as good as you!" announced the black kid proudly.

"How come?" asked Morrie.

"You've got a ranch house with a two-car garage and so do we."

A week later Carl Jr. declared a second time, "We're as good as you!"

"Is that so?"

"Uh huh. You've got a Plymouth station wagon and so do we."

Morrie nodded, and the two went on to school. But a week later, Carl Jr. announced, "We're *better* than you are!"

Morrie scowled. "How do you figure that?"

"There's only white people living next door to us!"

•

Luther and Jefferson were sharecroppers on adjoining pieces of land, and when his mule went lame, Luther went over to see if he could borrow Jefferson's donkey for the day.

"Sorry, Luther, but my boy rode that donkey to school," said Jefferson in response.

Just then a loud braying erupted from the barn behind the house. "That noise don't sound like it's coming from town," Luther pointed out, eyeing his neighbor suspiciously.

"Now just a dang minute!" Jefferson burst out. "You gonna take that donkey's word against mine?"

•

"Tell me, Mr. Loman," said the judge to the black man standing before the bench, "is your wife dependent on you?"

"She sure is, Your Honor," replied the defendant earnestly. "Why, if I didn't collect other folks' laundry and bring it home for her to do, she'd probably starve to death."

•

A white woman and her black housekeeper became pregnant at the same time, and had their babies on the same day. And about a year later, the white woman came running into the kitchen. "Maisie, Maisie," she cried happily, "little Bobbie said his first word!"

"He did?" responded the black baby from her play-pen in the corner. "What'd he say?"

IRAQI

What's the difference between the Iraqi Army and Ted Kennedy?
  Ted Kennedy has at least one confirmed kill.

•

Did you hear that Saddam Hussein's doing a movie for the Disney studio?
  It's called "Honey, I Scud the Yids."

•

What do Fred Flintstone and Saddam Hussein have in common?
  They both live next to rubble.

•

What do you do when an Iraqi soldier throws a hand-grenade at you?

Take out the pin and toss it back.

•

Hear about the remodelled Iraqi tanks?

They have one speed in forward, and four in reverse.

•

Did you hear Iraq and Kuwait are becoming a single country?

It's going to be called Irate.

•

How do you get eighty-seven network newspeople into a closet in Riyadh?

Tell them it's gasproof.

•

The Iraqi diplomat was outraged when the customs people at JFK Airport put him and his luggage through the

25

wringer. "New York is the asshole of the world!" he declared in disgust.

"Yessir," agreed the customs official. "Are you just passing through?"

●

A new horror movie's playing to packed houses in Saudi Arabia:

It's called *Iraqnaphobia*.

●

Did you hear they rezoned Baghdad into two districts . . .

. . . smoking and non-smoking.

●

How do you empty a Baghdad bingo parlor?

Call out "B-52."

●

What do you have when 30 Iraqi women are gathered in the same room?

A full set of teeth.

How many Iraqi soldiers does it take to change a light bulb?
  I give up!

•

Did you hear about the Saddam Hussein doll?
  Wind it up and it takes Ken and Barbie hostage at the gas pump.

•

What do you call an Iraqi soldier in the desert?
  A speed bump.

•

What did Hussein and Dukakis have in common?
  Neither could believe he was losing to Bush.

•

What do you call a bunch of Iraqi women walking into a bar?
  Incoming Scuds.

How about in a hot tub?
  Gorillas in the mist.

Why does it take Iraqi pilots half as long as American
pilots to learn to fly?
  They don't have to learn how to land.

What do Saddam Hussein and Little Miss Muffet have
in common?
  They both had Kurds in the way.

Did you hear about the Saddam Hussein condom?
  It's for the man who doesn't know when to pull out.

What's the name of the new department store in Baghdad?
  Target.

•

Did you know Desert Shield condoms came packaged in a camouflaged box with a special slogan?

"For Those who Want a Piece in the Middle East"

•

What's the difference between a Hoover vacuum cleaner and an Iraqi tank?

The Hoover has only one dirt bag.

•

How many Iraqis does it take to fire a Scud missile?

Three. One to load it, one to shoot it, and one to go home and watch CNN to see where it landed.

•

Why did the Iraqi pilots fly their planes to Iran?

There isn't a country called I Quit.

•

What's the national bird of Iraq?
  Duck.

•

What do you call an Iraqi with a sheep under one arm
and a goat under the other?
  Bisexual.

•

How about if he's only carrying one sheep?
  A pimp.

•

Why're the Americans nervous about Iraq entering the
Olympics?
  Half their armed forces can run faster than Ben John-
son, and none of them take steroids!

•

What's the difference between American and Iraqi
fighter pilots?

The American pilots break ground, and fly into the wind. . . .

•

Did you hear the new Iraqi anthem?
   "Onward Christian Soldiers . . ."

•

What's the difference between an Iraqi woman and a catfish?
   One has whiskers and smells bad; the other is a fish.

•

There's good news and bad news about Saddam Hussein's war crimes:
   The good news is that President Bush will put him on trial.
   The bad news is that the trial's being conducted by the Senate Ethics Committee.

•

Why are secondhand Iraqi weapons such a good deal?
   They've only been thrown down once.

Why don't Iraqis go out drinking any more?
  They got used to getting bombed at home.

•

What do Victor Kiam and Saddam Hussein have in common?
  A big mouth, a losing team, and no respect for bush.

•

Did you hear that Saddam Hussein won the toss?
  He elected to receive.

•

Know why he had his wife taken out and shot?
  He caught her drinking Busch beer and eating quail.

•

Did you know Hussein had a secret plan that would have won for sure?

He was going to take one thousand lawyers hostage and release them one at a time until we surrendered.

•

Saddam Hussein seems to be at it again. Last night he launched six Scuds at Israel . . . and caused over half a million dollars worth of urban renewal.

•

Do you know how an Iraqi mine detector works?
He puts his hand over his ears and walks forward, tapping his foot.

•

Have you tried the new beer called Scud Lite?
You can drink it all night, but it never hits the spot.

•

Do you know why Americans only have one wife, while Iraqis have several?
Americans get to see their wives naked before they marry them!

ETHNIC VARIEGATED

Mr. Kurosawa frequented a certain Greek restaurant at lunchtime because of their very tasty fried rice, which without fail he pronounced "flied lice." This provoked great hilarity amongst the waiters and proprietors of the restaurant, who would often actually gather around for the pleasure of cracking up at the Japanese man's diction. Finally Kurosawa's pride was so battered that he went to a special diction coach. And it was a proud man who came in the next month, strode up to the counter, and ordered, "One fried rice, please."

Unable to believe his ears, the Greek waiter asked, "Sir, would you repeat that, please?"

Flushing with rage, eyes bulging, Kurosawa screamed, "You heard what I said, you fluckin' Gleek!"

•

What do you call a guy who's half-Chinese and half-Polish?
Somedumfuk!

•

Did you know the Republic of Ireland is hard at work on a new airborne weapon?

They're calling it the Spud missile.

•

The elderly Russian tottered down to the store to fetch his family's ration of meat, only to be informed that there was none to be had. Furious, the old man raged at the butcher for several minutes, cursing the wretched state of affairs in Russia, the endless lines, the inevitable shortages. And on his way out of the store he was approached by a sinister fellow in dark glasses and a black leather trenchcoat.

"Be careful, comrade," cautioned the man in a low voice. "If you had made a scene like this a few years ago, you know what would have happened to you." He pointed an imaginary pistol at the old fellow's temple, pulled the trigger, then walked off.

"What happened, Pyotr?" asked the old man's wife seeing him return home empty-handed. "Did they run out of meat again?"

"It's worse than that," he replied glumly. "They've run out of bullets."

•

How does a Greek firing squad line up?

One behind the other.

American journalist: "In Kuwait, is sex considered work or play?"

Kuwaiti: "It must be play. If it were work, we'd hire a Pakistani to do it for us."

●

The investigation into the fire which had destroyed Biaggi's warehouse took almost a year. So when he received word that the case had finally been settled, Biaggi headed right over to his lawyer's office to collect the insurance claim. Once there, he was stunned by just how large a percentage the lawyer was retaining to cover his services.

"Face it, Mr. Biaggi," said the lawyer smoothly, "I've earned it, now haven't I?"

"Jesus," muttered the businessman under his breath, "you'd think *you* started the fire."

●

Did you hear what Ali Baba and the Forty Ethiopians do for a living?

They rob supermarkets.

●

Why are there so many Chinese people in the world?

If you don't know, you've obviously never tried to do your own shirts!

•

Three privates were taken prisoner by the rebel forces, who decided to have them flogged as a fearsome example for their enemies. Not being a heartless beast, however, the rebel commander asked each man if he wished to have anything applied to his back to make the punishment more bearable.

Private DiFiore, whose parents hailed from the Old Country, requested olive oil. It was poured on his back and he was whipped within an inch of his life.

Next came Private Czernak, who prided himself on being one tough son of a bitch and declared "I don't need nuttin'. Dat's one," announced the soldier calmly as the whip came crashing down on his back. "Dat's two," he continued after the second mighty whack. And he went on counting calmly, oblivious to the fact that his back was beginning to resemble raw hamburger meat.

Last came Private Feinstein, who had paid close attention. When the commander asked what he would like, Feinstein replied promptly, "On my back, I want Czernak."

•

How can you identify a Rumanian jet fighter in a snowstorm?

It's the one with chains on the propellers.

What would you call a male Chinese porn star?
  Dragon Willie!

•

Two Finns were nursing their aquavits at the bar in silence for almost an hour. Finally, one glumly noted, "You know, Kalevi, I've been thinking. It's a dog-eat-dog world."
  Kalevi thought this over for ten or fifteen minutes. "You may be right, Tuevo," he pronounced at long last. "Or it could be the other way around."

•

What do you call a member of the Irish Republican Army who only carries a snubnosed .38 and a switchblade?
  A pacifist.

•

Know why all the Greek soldiers were wearing black armbands last month?

Didn't you hear about the ship that went down with ten thousand cases of Vaseline?

•

An idealistic young doctor volunteered for two years' service with the Peace Corps. He was put in charge of a population-control program in a remote Nepalese hill town. It turned out to be impossible for the women to keep track of birth-control pills, so the doctor decided to concentrate on the use of condoms.

His first patient was a man whose wife had given birth to six children in as many years, and neither wanted more. The doctor explained how the sheaths worked, and that if he wore one conscientiously, his wife would not get pregnant. So he was surprised when the fellow's wife came in a month later, and found she was pregnant again.

"What happened?" he scolded. "All your husband had to do was keep the condom on—is that so difficult?"

"He try, he try very hard," stammered the poor woman, "but after three days he have to pee so bad he cut the end off."

•

Did you know they just discovered that the oil slick off Kuwait shouldn't be blamed on the Iraqis . . .

It was caused by the Italian navy taking a swim.

39

What happened in the United Nations when Iraq invaded Kuwait?

An hour later Switzerland declared itself neutral and Italy surrendered.

●

The young Irish bride made her first appointment with a gynecologist and told him of her and her husband's wish to start a family. "We've been trying for months now, Doctor Keith, and I don't seem to be able to get pregnant," she confessed miserably.

"I'm sure we'll solve the problem," the doctor reassured her. "If you'll just get up on the examining table and take off your underpants . . ."

"Well, all right, Doctor," agreed the young woman, blushing, "but I'd rather have my husband's baby."

●

Did you hear about this fabulous new diet?

It has two parts: 1) you can only eat bagels and lox; and 2) you have to live in Syria.

●

At the Congress of Nations a dispute broke out over the nationality of Adam and Eve.

"They were English," stated the British delegate, "because only an Englishman would have been such a gentleman as to give his own rib to make a woman."

"Mais non!" protested the French delegate. "Look at how elegant Adam was, despite his naked state. He was a Frenchman."

The Israeli delegate demurred, pointing out that the Bible clearly stated that the Creation occurred in the Holy Land. "So Adam and Eve were of the Chosen People; they were Jews."

The Russian shook his head. "Adam and Eve could only have been Russian," he maintained, "because only a Russian could eat so poorly, dress so badly, and still call it Paradise."

•

Did you know Ireland was all set to send a tank convoy to the Gulf . . .

. . . but they couldn't find a designated driver.

•

When his spacecraft experienced technical difficulties, the alien was forced to make an emergency landing on Earth. He landed in an empty lot and his eyes lit up when he spotted bagels in the window of a deli on the corner. Scuttling inside, he said politely, "Excuse me, I would like to purchase two of those small wheels."

"Those aren't wheels," said Goldfarb, the proprietor, looking the strange customer over carefully. "They're bagels."

The alien nodded politely. "What would the price be for two wheels for my spacecraft?"

"Listen, Greenface, they aren't wheels, they're bagels. They're for eating."

The alien calmly persisted. "May I purchase two wheels, please?"

"You gotta see for yourself, don't you buddy?" Gold-farb handed a fresh bagel to the little green man. "Eat, eat!"

"You know," commented the alien after eating the whole bagel, "this would go great with cream cheese."

●

How many American businessmen does it take to screw in a light bulb?

Two. One to hold the bulb, and the other to ask their Japanese banker which way to turn it.

●

A passerby watched the progress of two workmen from the Department of Parks as they moved down a Moscow street. One stopped every twenty feet to dig a hole, the second filled it in as soon as he was done, and they

42

moved on to the next site. Finally overcome by curiosity, the observer asked what in heaven's name they were doing. "You certainly aren't accomplishing anything," she pointed out.

"You don't understand at all," protested the first worker indignantly. "We are usually a team of three: I dig the hole, Sergei plants the tree, and Vladimir packs the dirt back in. Today Sergei is home with the flu, but that doesn't mean Vladimir and I get to stop working, now does it?"

HOMOSEXUAL

How can you spot a tough lesbian bar?
Even the pool table doesn't have any balls.

•

The desk sergeant was very understanding when the eminent scholar called up at two in the morning, his voice trembling. "This . . . this *brute* broke into my house," he explained, "and came right up to my bedroom, and positively ripped the bedcovers off me. He looked me over in the vilest, most humiliating way you could imagine, Officer, and then he pulled down his pants and revealed this incredibly huge penis."

"That sounds awful, Professor Pilkington," said the policeman soothingly.

"And then he shoved the entire thing into my mouth, until I thought I'd choke," the professor went on, voice quavering, "and then he rolled me over and penetrated me until I was seeing stars. Why, I thought I was going to be torn in two."

"Gee, that's really terrible."

"Oh, but that's not all. When he was finally done, he urinated all over me—he even made me drink some." At this, Pilkington broke down completely.

"Now hang in there, Professor," said the sergeant reassuringly. "I'll get a couple of my men over there right away. You give us a good description and we'll scour the town for that sick son-of-a-bitch."

"Oh, that isn't really necessary," said the professor, brightening considerably. "He's in the shower now. Why don't you just send that squad car over in the morning?"

•

What's the difference between a priest and a homosexual?

The way they pronounce "A-men."

•

Why did the fag strip naked and tie a string to his dick?

He was going to a costume party as a pull toy.

•

Two Marines got off guard duty and decided to head into town for a quick drink. As they approached a streetlight, Malone looked over and whistled admiringly. "Quite a bulge you've got in your pants, Mancini."

"The only place in town serving drinks this late is a gay bar," the soldier explained curtly.

"So, you looking for some action?" his buddy teased. "What's with the bulge?"

Mancini snarled, "I stuffed two handgrenades in my shorts. First queer that tries to feel me up gets his hand blown off."

•

Did you hear about the horrible new disease transmitted via lesbian sex?

It's called MAIDS.

•

Who did the gay guy hire to find out how he'd contracted AIDS?

Dick Tracer.

•

What do you get from a Puerto Rican fag?

Foreign AIDS.

Phillips fancied himself quite the ladies' man, so when his cruise ship went down in a storm and he found himself stranded on a desert island with six women, he couldn't believe his good fortune. They agreed quickly that each woman would have one night a week with the only man. Phillips threw himself into the arrangement with gusto, working even on his day off, but as the weeks stretched into months, he found himself looking forward to that day of rest more and more eagerly.

One afternoon he was sitting on the beach and wishing for some more men to share his duties when he caught sight of a life raft bobbing in the waves. Phillips swam out to the guy, pulled the raft to shore, and did a little jig of happiness. "You can't believe how happy I am to see you," he cried.

The new fellow eyed him up and down and cooed, "You're a sight for sore eyes, too, you gorgeous thing."

"Shit," sighed Phillips. "There go my Sundays."

•

Why did the gay shepherd go broke?
His herd died of AIDS.

•

What's worse than your doctor telling you you have AIDS?
Your mother telling you.

The compulsive gambler walked into a gay bar, ordered a drink, and struck up a conversation with a fellow at the bar. When his companion went to take a leak, the gambler turned to the guy on the other side of him and said boldly, "I bet you fifty dollars you've got terrible hemorrhoids."

Knowing this wasn't the case, the fag readily agreed to the bet, stood up, and pulled down his pants. The gambler shoved a broomstick up his ass, didn't find a single hemorrhoid, promptly handed over the fifty dollars, and headed for the bathroom. The winner sat back down on his barstool and delightedly recounted the story to his friend on his return.

To his surprise, his friend paled. "That son-of-a-bitch!" he cried. "Just ten minutes ago he bet me a hundred dollars he'd have a broomstick shoved up your ass in five minutes!"

•

Did you hear about the gay soldier who put shoe polish in his Vaseline . . .

. . . so he could rise and shine?

•

The dentist was startled when an obvious homosexual pranced into his examining room, reclined in the chair, and pulled out his dick. "What the hell are you doing?" the dentist blustered. "I'm a *dentist!*"

"I know, Dr. Ridley, I know," said the guy soothingly. "There's a tooth in there."

•

What does a gay have after getting gang-banged?
   A full moon.

•

What's the difference between a fag and a refrigerator?
   A refrigerator doesn't fart when you take out the meat.

•

What's the difference between AIDS and golf?
   In golf, one bad hole won't kill you.

•

The drill sergeant lost no time endearing himself to his new bunch of recruits. Walking down the center aisle of the barracks, he bellowed at the boys on his right, "You're all shit-ass, good-for-nothing excuses for men."

Turning to the ones on his left, he howled, "And *you* limp-wristed cocksuckers are the sorriest sons of bitches I've ever set eyes on!"

When a meek-looking man got to his feet, the DI spun around to confront him. "You gotta problem?" he demanded belligerently.

"Oh, no sir," replied the new recruit timidly. "It's just that I'm on the wrong side of the room."

•

Did you hear about the new gay football team?

It's going to be called the San Francisco 69'ers.

•

What happens in a gay Western?

All the good guys are hung.

•

What did one homosexual say to the other as they walked past a gay bar?

"Say, you want to go in there and get shitfaced?"

HANDICAPPED

What do a hemophiliac and a virgin have in common?
  One prick and it's all over.

•

"Hadley, I know you have always been embarrassed by
the fact that Hadley Junior was born mentally retarded,
and have done your best to ignore his existence," said
Mrs. Withington firmly, "but today is his tenth birthday
and you owe him some sort of appropriate gesture."

Mr. Withington set aside his newspaper and nodded
in agreement. "I suppose you're right. Have Nurse
Hawkins wheel him into my study when I get back from
the country club."

At the appointed hour, Hadley Junior sat in front of
his father, who took a deep breath and began, "Happy
Birthday . . . and I suppose the time is right for a
man-to-thing chat."

What's the difference between an alcoholic and a drunk?

A drunk doesn't have to go to meetings.

•

"Ladies and gentlemen," queried the medical-school teacher, "today I would like you to consider what could be done for a child born without a penis. Yes, Mr. Dennis?"

"I'd wait till she was sixteen and give her one," responded the student brightly.

•

Did you hear that things were getting so tough at the recruiting centers . . .

. . . that they started accepting midgets pasted together?

•

You probably already know a leper's two favorite songs ("Put Your Head on My Shoulders" and "I Wanna Hold

Your Hand"), but what about his second and third favorites?

"I'm All Shook Up" and "Falling to Pieces!"

•

"Great news, Mr. Oscarson," the psychiatrist reported. "After eighteen months of therapy, I can pronounce you finally and completely cured of your kleptomania. You'll never be trapped by such desires again."

"Gee, that's great, Doc," said the patient with a sigh of relief.

"And just to prove it, I want you to stop off at Sears on the way home and walk the length of the store. You'll see—you'll feel no temptation to shoplift whatsoever."

"Oh Doctor, how can I ever thank you?"

"Well," suggested the doctor, "if you do have a relapse, I could use a microwave."

•

What do you call the veteran whose lower legs were blown off by a land mine?

Neil.

•

How about the kid with no arms and no legs and a harelip lying on the bottom of the bathtub?
  Dwayne.

•

How about the girl with no arms and no legs who never comes out of the closet?
  Heidi.

•

Or the one who still gets a thrill out of making hamburgers?
  Wendy.

•

More than anything else, dim Dougie wanted to be a cowboy. He clearly didn't have enough brains to succeed at any sort of clerical work, but he was a sturdy boy, so a local rancher took pity and decided to give him a chance.
  "I've sure you've seen one of these," he began, putting a comforting arm around Dougie's shoulders and showing him a long rope. "It's a lariat—we use it to catch cows."

"Okay, sir," said Dougie, brow furrowed in concentration. "And what do you use for bait?"

•

What's Kurt Waldheimer Disease?
It's like Alzheimer's Disease, except you only forget war crimes.

•

How did Helen Keller rip her arm off?
She tried to read the speed limit sign at 55 mph.

•

Didrickson lined up for his first Army sick call. While he was waiting for his name to be called, the private to his left leaned over and said conspiratorially, "I hear these doctors are really tough. They don't want any malingerers, you know. A guy in my unit came in complaining about his corns, and the surgeon cut three toes off."

Didrickson blanched, and turned even paler when the guy on his right nodded in confirmation. "Listen to *this:* a guy in my barracks came in with an earache and came back with a bandage where his ear used to be."

That did it. The new recruit jumped to his feet and yelped, "I've gotta get out of here—I've got the clap."

What's the difference between a tree and someone who's had leprosy for ten years?
The tree has limbs.

•

Know why the Siamese twins moved to London?
So the other one could drive.

•

What do you say to a woman with no arms and no legs?
"Nice tits!"

RELIGIOUS

What did Buddha say to the hot dog vendor?
  "Make me one with everything."

•

When the convent was returning from its annual retreat in the mountains, the bus went over an embankment and four nuns were instantly killed. They materialized at the Pearly Gates, where St. Peter asked the first sister whether she had sinned during her time on earth. She blushed and confessed to having kissed a boy the day before taking her vows.

"Wash your lips in the holy water," ordered St. Peter, "and proceed into Heaven. And you, Sister, have you sinned?"

The second nun blushed deeply and stammered, "St. Peter, I once touched a man's penis."

"Wash your hands in the holy water and you shall be

57

cleansed and admitted into Heaven." He turned expectantly to the remaining nuns, only to be startled by the sight of both women fighting for position in front of the font of holy water. "Ladies, ladies," he remonstrated. "What in Heaven's name is going on?"

"It's like this, St. Peter," replied one of the nuns. "I was last in line, but don't you think I should be allowed to gargle in the holy water before Bridget has to sit in it?"

•

Three clerics in an ecumenical community were charged with gambling with the Bingo pool. "You three should be setting moral examples for the community, not degrading them," scolded the judge. "How do you plead?"

"Not guilty," said the priest.

"Not guilty," said the minister.

"Not guilty," said the rabbi. "Who could I have been gambling with?"

•

What's white and streaks across the nighttime sky?
    The coming of the Lord.

•

An ecclesiastical conference was housed at a Holiday Inn for the weekend, and the hotel manager was aghast to learn that the clergymen had accidentally been served a watermelon spiked with vodka. Nervously he hovered by the door to the dining room. "Well?" he whispered to the headwaiter. "Any complaints? Any reaction at all?"

"Relax, Mr. Smith," said the waiter. "They're all too busy slipping the seeds into their pockets."

•

What do you call the Pope's bowel movement?
   Holy shit.

•

Two aging prostitutes decided they'd had enough of the hard life on the streets, and joined the Salvation Army. Well, Yvonne really took to the new life, but Rhonda had her moments of missing the old, wild days. After a couple of months she admitted to her friend that she just had to go get drunk and laid. And off she went.

It being a Saturday night, Yvonne held her street service in a particularly seamy part of town. And she was just hitting her stride as Rhonda came staggering by with her arm around an equally drunken man. "Friends," preached Yvonne from her Salvation Army soapbox, hitting her stride, "I used to be in the arms of sailors, I used to be in the arms of soldiers, I used to be in the arms of Marines . . . but now I'm in the arms of the Lord."

"Way to go, Yvonne," yelled Rhonda from the back of the crowd, "fuck 'em all!"

•

Smith was a man of cold facts, a scientist, a computer jock, and a confirmed atheist. He became somewhat obsessed with the desire to prove the truth as he saw it. So he mortgaged his house and sold his car in order to put a downpayment on the most powerful computer commercially available. Then Smith plugged it into every data bank in the world, accessed every library in the United States and Europe, and had the machine scan every book published since the invention of the printing press.

Finally Smith sat down at the console, took a deep breath, and typed, "Is there a God?"

The monitor flickered, the hard drives clicked, and up on the screen came the words, "There is now."

•

What was the name of the Roman soldier who nailed Jesus to the cross?

Spike.

•

Jesus and Moses went golfing, and were about even until they reached the fifteenth hole, a par five. Both balls landed about twenty feet from the edge of a little pond that stood between them and the hole. Moses took out a 5-wood and landed his ball in excellent position. Jesus took out a 5-iron.

"Hang on, hang on," cautioned Moses. "Use a wood —you'll never make it."

"If Arnold Palmer can make that shot with a 5-iron, so can I," said Jesus. His ball landed in the middle of the lake. Moses parted the waters, retrieved the ball, and sighed when he saw Jesus still holding the 5-iron.

"If Arnold Palmer can make that shot with a 5-iron, so can I," maintained Jesus. Again Moses had to part the waters to retrieve the ball. By this time there were a number of people waiting to play through, and Moses said firmly, "Listen, Jesus, I'm not fetching the ball another time. Use a wood."

Jesus, however, still insisted, "If Arnold Palmer can make that shot with a 5-iron, so can I." *Splash!*

Moses shook his head. "I told you, I'm not budging. Get it yourself." So Jesus walked off across the water towards where the ball had landed.

At this, the onlookers gaped in astonishment. One came over to Moses and stammered, "I can't believe my eyes—that guy must think he's Jesus Christ!"

In response, Moses shook his head gloomily. "He *is* Jesus Christ. He *thinks* he's Arnold Palmer."

•

The congregation liked their new clergyman but were somewhat puzzled by his speaking style. His first sermon ran only eight minutes; the following Sunday he spoke for forty-five minutes; the third week he rattled on for almost an hour and a half. That was enough for the board to summon him in for a little chat.

To their relief, Wilkerson had a ready explanation. "The Saturday before my first sermon I'd had the last of my teeth pulled and my mouth was terribly sore. But by the time a week had gone by, I'd gotten used to my new dentures." Here the minister paused and blushed deeply. "And as for last Sunday . . . well, I'm afraid that I picked up my wife's set of teeth by mistake."

●

What do you get when you cross a Jehovah's Witness with a Hell's Angel?

Someone who knocks on your door at 7:30 on a Saturday morning and tells you to go fuck yourself.

FEMALE

Why did they send so many women with PMS to the Gulf?

They fight like animals, and they retain water for four days.

•

How come you can't trust a woman?

How can you trust someone who bleeds for five days and doesn't die?

•

When Roger met Ruby in a bar one night, he thought she was gorgeous, and he remained intrigued even after she'd confessed to having an incredible foot fetish. So he accepted her invitation to come back to her place, and obligingly fucked her with his big toe.

A few days later he woke up with his toe swollen and throbbing. He hobbled over to the doctor, where he was told he had syphilis of the foot. Roger admitted he'd never known such a condition existed. "Is it rare, Doc?"

"Fairly, but I've seen weirder," the doctor told him. "Just this morning a lady came in with athlete's cunt."

●

Hear about the woman who sent out fifteen hundred perfumed Valentines signed "Guess who?"

She's a divorce lawyer.

●

Maureen packed a whole rainbow of beautiful negligees for her honeymoon, figuring on one for each night. But as it turned out, her husband liked the whole variety that very first night. The second night there was no response, nor the third, nor the fourth, and so on, until, on the last night of the honeymoon, Maureen came to bed in black.

"Gee, honey, how come the black?" asked the new husband groggily, as he had been sound asleep.

"I'm mourning a dead cock," explained Maureen.

●

What do you call a prostitute who works a thruway exit?
  A toll-house cookie.

·

What's another term for a gynecologist's office?
  The Womb Room.

·

An awesomely homely coed wanted to go home to New Jersey for Thanksgiving, and since she didn't have much money she decided to hitchhike. But no one would stop to pick her up. *Zooooom. Whooosh.* The cars just sped on by down the Interstate.

After several disappointing hours, the coed hiked her skirt up to mid-thigh in the hopes of enticing some lonely male to pick her up. *Vrooooom. Whooooosh.* The traffic sped past.

Tired and hungry, the coed opened her blouse and flashed a little tit. *Zoooom. Vrooom. Whooosh.* No response whatsoever; in fact, if anything, the traffic seemed actually to be picking up speed.

That did it. Exhausted and furious, the coed stripped off all her clothes. Stark naked, she moved back to the edge of the highway just as a gang of Hell's Angels roared into view. Gunning their motorcycles in a deafening roar, the men pulled into a circle around the girl, got off their bikes, and gang-dressed her.

What's a hooker's favorite drink?
A Penis Colada!

⚫

Harvey walked into the whorehouse and asked the manager if they had a special of the day. "As a matter of fact, we have three specials, sir," the manager informed him smoothly. "We have the sixty-niner, the straight-up job, and Hurricane Gussy."

"Hmmm," mused Harvey, "I've had the straight-up job, and I've heard about the sixty-niner, so I guess I'll take Hurricane Gussy."

"Room Seventeen," instructed the manager, pointing the way.

Harvey went into the room, stripped, and lay down on the bed, and pretty soon a fat woman came in, undressed, and started doing what she was supposed to do —until suddenly she farted loudly.

"Look, lady, I love what you're doing, but what was that for?"

"I'm Hurricane Gussy," explained the fat woman calmly, "and that was the tropical wind."

They started up again where they'd left off, and Harvey was having a fine time until the woman stood up and peed in his face.

"Jesus, lady," sputtered Harvey, "what was *that* for?"

"I'm Hurricane Gussy," she reminded him, "and that was the tropical rain."

So they got back to what they'd been doing, and Harvey was really enjoying himself, when suddenly the woman grabbed his head, shoved it between her breasts, and started shaking them violently back and forth.

"I give up," gasped Harvey coming up for air.

"I'm Hurricane Gussy," said the fat woman with a smile, "and that was the coconuts falling from the trees."

●

Why couldn't the WAVE get pregnant during the gale at sea?

The seamen kept falling to the floor.

●

A man died and went to Hell for his sins. As the Devil was leading him off to the pool of fire and brimstone that was to be his to fry in for eternity, he caught sight of a hideously ugly colleague from his office passionately making love to a gorgeous woman.

Under his breath the man cursed the injustice of it all. "Here I am, soon to be roasting in agony, and that guy gets to dally with a beautiful babe."

The Devil turned on him and roared, "And just who are you to question that woman's punishment?"

●

Why did the promiscuous girl have a heart like the United States Army?

It was open to any man between the ages of eighteen and thirty-five.

•

The real-estate mogul was delighted by the comely new receptionist, and proceeded to turn all of his charms upon her. Within a few weeks, however, he grew extremely displeased at her growing tardiness. "Listen, baby," he roared one morning, "we may have gone to bed together a few times, but who said you could start coming in late?"

The secretary replied sweetly, "My lawyer."

•

Hear the one about the lovesick gynecologist who looked up an old girlfriend . . . ?

•

It took three years for Shelley to wise up to the fact that going to a psychiatrist wasn't doing her any good at all: now she was broke, when to start with she'd only been cracked.

What do you call a woman pilot with VD?
  An aircraft carrier.

•

Mrs. Swindon declined to serve on the jury because she was not a believer in capital punishment and didn't want her beliefs to get in the way of the trial. "But madam," said the public defender, who had taken a liking to her kind face and calm demeanor, "this is not a murder trial. It is merely a civil lawsuit being brought by a wife against her husband. He gambled away the twelve thousand dollars he'd promised to spend on a sable coat for her birthday."

  "Hmmm," mused Mrs. Swindon. "Okay, I'll serve. I could be wrong about capital punishment."

•

Did you hear what happened to the woman who swallowed a razor blade on Monday?
  By Thursday she'd given herself a hysterectomy, castrated her husband, circumcised her boyfriend, and given the priest a harelip.

•

Why did the dentist spend his entire vacation in a whorehouse?

He wanted bigger cavities to drill.

•

"Dr. Bernard completely cured my hemorrhoids," Betty informed the other girls in the secretarial pool. "How'd he do it? First he had me bend over, of course, and then he put one hand on my shoulder and stuck the other up my. . . . Hang on a sec." Betty's face screwed up in concentration, and then she went on, "Yeah, that's it: Dr. Bernard put his right hand on my shoulder and stuck his left up. . . ."

Betty paled. "Wait just a minute!" she gasped. "He had *both* hands on my shoulders!"

•

Did you hear about the sex maniac who had asthma?

He could only catch his breath in snatches.

MALE

Why do men have more brains than dogs?
  So they won't hump women's legs at cocktail parties.

•

A platoon of Green Berets was temporarily billeted near a select women's college. The commanding officer immediately made an appointment with the dean of students to alert her to the dangers of the situation. "My men have been out on maneuvers for over six months and are pretty damn . . . uh, hungry for female companionship," he informed her. "I advise that you lock the dorms at night and keep the campus gates guarded at all times."

"May I remind you of the extraordinary reputation of the College of the Sacred Heart?" responded the dean condescendingly. "Our girls have it up here." And she tapped her temple with her index finger.

"If you say so, ma'am," said the colonel politely. "But

let me assure you that it makes no difference where they have it—my men will find it."

•

"Doc," said LaRusso, "I got nine kids and the wife's expecting again. How do I stop the stork?"

The doctor replied, "Shoot it in the air!"

•

The Bergs went over to the local Oldsmobile dealership to pick out a new car. No sooner had gorgeous Mrs. Berg set foot on the car lot than the salesman's jaw dropped. He couldn't take his eyes off her.

Never one to pass up a chance at a bargain, Berg pulled the salesman aside. "She's really something, eh?" he commented with a sly smile.

The salesman nodded dumbly, eyes glued to Mrs. Berg's cleavage.

"Tell you what," Berg proposed. "You've got a back room here, right? Let's take her back there, and if you can do everything I can do, I'll pay double for that convertible in the corner of the lot. If you can't, I get the car for nothing."

The salesman agreed enthusiastically, his gaze dropping to Mrs. Berg's perfect, miniskirted ass. As soon as the door was closed, Berg pulled up his wife's t-shirt and started fondling the luscious melons that popped out. The salesman followed suit energetically.

Next Berg circled her navel with his tongue. The salesman licked her whole stomach, trying not to drool.

Next Berg pulled up her teeny-weeny skirt, feeling the soft down of her inner thighs. The salesman followed, the slight tang of her pussy almost driving him insane.

Next Berg pulled out his pecker and folded it in half. The salesman sighed. "What color car d'you want?"

●

Why's beauty more important than brains for a woman?

Because plenty of men are stupid, but not very many are blind.

●

Hector decided to treat himself to a trip to the whorehouse, and turned to catch the hooker's expression when he dropped his pants—his dong was eighteen inches long.

"Oh my God," gasped the poor girl, "you're not putting *that* inside me! I'll kiss it, I'll lick it . . ."

"No way," Hector broke in. "I can do that myself."

●

The horny midget found that the best way to make time with women was to be direct about it. So he went up to the tallest, blondest woman at the party and said, "Hey, honey, whaddaya say to a little fuck?"

She looked down at him and promptly replied, "Hello, you little fuck!"

•

Farmer Swenson came into town for market day, and sold everything but one goose by noon, so he decided to treat himself to an afternoon at the movies. But the girl at the ticket counter took one look at the goose and said, "You can't take that bird in here."

Swenson went around the corner, stuck the bird under his belt, and went into the movies. Everything was fine through the first couple of gunfights, but eventually the goose started getting restless. So Swenson took pity on it and opened his fly so the bird could stick its head out for some fresh air.

Two little old ladies sitting next to the farmer were also enjoying the matinee. "Minnie," whispered one to the other, "you seen one, you seen 'em all—but this one's eating my popcorn!"

•

Why did the little boy think his father had two dicks?

He saw him use a small one to pee with, and a big one for brushing the babysitter's teeth.

Harry noticed he was running low on rubbers, so he stopped by the local drug store. "What size?" asked the pharmacist's assistant sweetly.

When he admitted he wasn't sure of his size, she led him into the back room, lifted her skirt, and told him to enter her. He was delighted to oblige.

"Size six," she informed him after a moment or two, "now take it out. How many please?"

Harry bought a dozen, and on the way down the street he ran into his friend Alan, to whom he eagerly recounted the whole episode. Needless to say, Alan rushed right in to place an order. "I'm afraid I don't know my size," he told the salesgirl.

So she led him into the back room and repeated the procedure. "Size seven sir, now take it out. How many, please?"

But Alan plugged away, undeterred, until he came. "None, thanks," he told her, zipping up his fly and smiling broadly. "Just came in for a fitting."

•

The only survivor of a shipwreck, Pierre washed ashore on a desert island. He managed to find food and water, and didn't mind the solitude, but he grew horny as hell, so when a sheep walked down the beach one day, he jumped at it. Pierre led the beast back to his hut, but just as he was starting to get it on, a dog ran out of the jungle and began to attack him. And in trying to beat the dog away, Pierre had to let the sheep go.

In the weeks that followed the sheep appeared regularly, but every time Pierre tried to get romantic with her, the dog materialized and attacked him viciously.

A few months later a lovely woman washed up on the shore. She was half drowned, but Pierre was able to resuscitate her, and when she came to, she was grateful beyond words. "You saved my life," she sobbed. "I would have drowned. How may I repay you? I'll do anything, just name it. . . . Anything!"

Pierre grabbed the sheep and ordered, "Hold that dog."

●

Terry and Larry go to the movies. "Gee, you're cold tonight," she whispers.

Larry whispers back, "You're holding my Popsicle."

●

The nudist colony offered woodworking as one of the activities, so Mike decided to try his hand at it. He was busy whittling away when his knife slipped and almost cut off his penis.

"Jesus, Mike," shrieked his pecker, turning to look up at him, "we've had our share of fistfights, but I never thought you'd pull a knife on me!"

Henderson was enjoying a few at his local pub when a man joined him at the bar, swaying back and forth as he stood there. It started to get on Henderson's nerves, so finally he turned to the stranger and asked, "What's with you, all this lurching back and forth? Can't you stand still?"

"I was with the Merchant Marines for nineteen years," the fellow explained genially, "and the roll of the sea kind of got in my blood."

"Is that so? Well, I've got fourteen kids," sputtered Henderson, starting to pump his hips energetically back and forth, "and I don't stand like this!"

DeFiore took up golf and was very proud of his new hobby. "Why, last week my boss and I played golf in the snow," he boasted to his buddy.

"Yeah? You have to paint your balls?" asked Maxwell.

"Nah," he replied offhandedly. "We wore long johns."

Norton goes into the men's room and takes a seat in a stall. Fifteen minutes later, nothing's happened. His pal

Dawson comes in and takes the next stall, and right away Norton hears, *Ploop!*

"You sure are lucky," grunts Norton.

"Lucky?" moans Dawson. "That was my watch."

•

What's a lawyer's definition of a bachelor?

Some son-of-a-bitch who's cheated a deserving woman out of her divorce settlement.

•

Nate was in a nasty accident, and broke so many bones that it was necessary for him to be placed in a body cast, with all four limbs and his neck immobilized in traction. And during his lengthy hospitalization, he had to be fed rectally.

The attending nurse felt especially sorry for him when his birthday came around, so she decided to give him a special treat: some ice cream through the food tube. But she'd barely left the room before Nate's screams of, "Nurse! Nurse!" echoed down the corridor.

Rushing back in, she cried, "What's the matter? Is it too cold? I'm so sorry—"

"No, no, no," Nate howled back. "I *hate* rum raisin!"

CRUELTY TO ANIMALS

The Australian tourist couldn't wait for shore leave in the Big Apple. He lost no time in picking up a hooker and bringing her back to his hotel room. Asking her to undress, he proceeded to lean the bed up against the wall and toss every other article of furniture out the window.

"What on Earth are you planning to do with me?" asked the hooker nervously.

"I'm not exactly sure, ma'am," answered the Australian, "but if it's anything like it is with a kangaroo, we'll need all the room we can get."

•

What do you call a dog with three legs?
Tippy.

•

Mr. Quackenbush was a devoted gardener, and the neighbor's yappy little dog used to drive him nuts by digging in his vegetable garden and peeing on his flowers. But one day the neighbor on the other side noticed the old gent working outside with an unusually contented look on his face. "How come?" she inquired.

"I solved the dog problem," confessed Quackenbush in a stage whisper. "Cut its tail off."

The neighbor was puzzled. "What good's that going to do?"

"At the neck."

•

What's the difference between a French poodle humping your leg and a pit bull humping your leg?

You let the pit bull finish.

•

Who does a gay yeti search for?

Bigdick.

•

The Special Forces commando had commandeered a Kuwaiti camel for a special mission, but suddenly the beast stopped dead in its tracks. Despite a stream of physical and verbal abuse, the camel refused to take another step. The fellow was just standing there, cursing furiously, when a Jeep appeared over the crest of the sand dune. "What's the problem?" asked the WAC at the wheel.

"My camel won't go," admitted the embarrassed commando.

The WAC jumped out, reached between the camel's rear legs for a moment—and the animal took off like a shot.

"Impressive," he conceded. "What did you do?"

"Just tickled his testicles," she replied with a grin. "Works every time."

The commando turned his back, dropped his pants, and said, "Well, you better tickle mine, 'cause I've gotta catch him!"

•

What animal has an asshole halfway up its back?
   A police horse.

•

How does an elephant get off on an oak tree?
   He sits on an acorn and waits.

•

A koala bear took a trip to New York, and while he was wandering around the theater district a hooker picked him up. He was happy to follow her up to a rented room, where they had the most incredible sex of her life. But right afterwards, the bear got up and headed for the door.

"Hey," yelled the hooker, "you haven't paid me!"

The koala looked confused, so she threw him a dictionary and told him to look up "prostitute."

The koala read out loud, "One who engages in the sexual act for fees." Then he tossed the dictionary right back and instructed her to look up "koala."

"Hmmmm," read the hooker, "an animal who eats shoots and leaves. . . ."

•

What do you call two skunks in the sixty-nine position?
Odor eaters.

•

Observing the way her neighbor's cat was tearing around the neighborhood, Libby called the neighbor up.

"Yeah, well, he's just been neutered," explained the cat's owner matter-of-factly, "and he's running around cancelling engagements."

•

How do you find a foxhole?
    Lift its tail.

•

"Gee, I hope the weather's going to be good this weekend," confided the kangaroo to her fellow homemaker. "It really wears me out when the kids have to play inside."

•

Did you hear about the veterinarian and the taxidermist who went into business together?
    Their slogan was, "Either Way, You Get Your Pet Back."

•

The fussy old woman telephoned the vet one day and insisted that he pay a house call on her beloved cat FooFoo. "Her tummy's getting bigger and bigger," she explained. "I'm afraid it's a tumor, Doctor."
    It took the doctor about two seconds to confirm that little FooFoo was knocked up.
    "It can't be!" protested the old woman. "Why, FooFoo never even *sees* another cat. In fact she only leaves the house in her carrying case when I bring her to

the Kitty Salon for her shampoo. How could she be pregnant?"

Just then a big tomcat strolled into the room. "What about him?" asked the vet.

"Impossible!" she cried. "That's her brother!"

•

What do you call a virgin parrot?
Polly-unsaturated.

•

Which animal wears the biggest brassiere?
A Z-bra.

•

Fernandez had made a lot of money in show business as a ventriloquist and decided to retire as a gentleman farmer. He selected a farm he liked, but found it somewhat overpriced, so he decided to have some fun with the farmer as they toured the outbuildings.

"How's the barn holding up?" he asked, turning towards the swaybacked horse in a corner stall.

"The roof leaks, and the tractor's thirty-five years old," replied the horse. The farmer, not realizing it was Fernandez throwing his voice, turned pale.

"Mooo," said the cow in answer to the ventriloquist's next question. "My stall's falling apart and the feed's all moldy."

The farmer started to quake.

Next were the chickens. "Need a new coop, holes in the wire," they cackled.

"Just a dang minute," interrupted the farmer, grabbing his prospective buyer by the shoulders. "Don't talk to the sheep—they lie."

•

What's brown and fuzzy and lays in the forest?

Smokey the hooker.

•

What can a duck do that a goose can't and a lawyer should?

Stick his bill up his ass.

•

"Vernon, where's your homework?" Miss Martin looked down sternly at the little boy and held out her hand.

"My dog ate it," was his solemn response.

"Vernon, I've been a teacher for eighteen years. Do you really expect me to believe that?"

"It's true, Miss Martin, I swear," insisted the boy. "I had to force him, but he ate it!"

CELEBRITIES

What do you do when you have Saddam Hussein, Muammar Khaddafi, and Al Sharpton in one room, but you only have two bullets?

Shoot Sharpton twice, to make sure he's dead.

•

What does Sinead O'Connor do after she combs her hair?

Pulls up her pants.

•

Did you hear General Foods is bringing out a new cereal named after Washington D.C's ex-mayor?

It's called Crack-n-Barry.

Did you know Marion Barry was arrested in Philadelphia too?

They found him trying to steal the crack out of the Liberty Bell.

•

What's eight inches long and hangs in front of an asshole?

Dan Quayle's tie.

•

What does Oprah Winfrey's husband say when he's in the mood to make love?

"How now, brown cow?"

•

Did you hear Jane Fonda's going to Yugoslavia on a goodwill mission?

The good news is that Ted Kennedy's driving her to the airport.

•

Did you hear the Secret Service's new orders?
    If anyone shoots Bush, they shoot Quayle.

•

Why are Michael Jackson's new lips such an advantage?
    They don't flap when he sings.

•

Have you read Joe Biden's new job résumé?
    Yeah, I don't have all night to stay up and read it
either.

•

What did Ted Bundy and Leonard Bernstein have in
common?
    They were both excellent conductors.

•

What was Yeltsin's first question to Bush at their first
meeting?
    "Why did you marry your mother?"

Why are the Rangers changing their name to the Tampons?

Because they're only good for one period, and they have no second string.

•

Why will history decide Ronald Reagan was a great actor?

Look at the way he played President for eight years.

•

Did you know Rob Lowe's shooting a new movie?

There's no title or script yet, just a location: Motel 16.

•

What did Rock Hudson say to Sammy Davis Jr. when they met on the other side?

"Gotta watch out for those butts—they'll get you whether you smoke 'em or poke 'em."

•

Arnold Schwarzenegger has a long one; Bush has a short one; the Pope has one but never uses it; Madonna doesn't have one at all. What is it?

A last name.

•

What do you get when you cross a karate expert with a tree?

Spruce Lee.

•

Did you hear about Zsa Zsa Gabor's new fragrance?

It's called "Conviction"—you just slap it on.

•

One day the Lone Ranger and Tonto rode into town for supplies. Tonto stayed outside the general store with the horses, but a north wind was blowing and he got pretty chilled. He started rubbing his hands together, and when that didn't work he started jogging in place, which didn't really warm him up either, so Tonto began running in a circle around the horses.

The proprietor of the store looked out his window and caught sight of this peculiar behavior. "Say, buddy," he asked, "are those your horses parked out front?"

"Sure are," answered the Lone Ranger. "Why do you ask?"

"Well, you left your injun runnin'."

•

Who designed the female genitals?

Spike Lee. Who else would make it short, black, bushy, and with big lips?

•

Why haven't they cremated Colonel Sanders yet?

They can't decide whether to do him regular or extra-crispy.

•

What the difference between Roseanne Barr and a Hell's Angel?

The motorcycle.

•

What happened when Jesse Jackson looked up his family tree?

A monkey peed on him.

Oprah Winfrey explained to the fancy diet doctor that Tom Brokaw was looking for a new co-anchor and that she was desperate to get the job. "But I've got to drop some weight, Dr. Borgman," she elaborated, "and I understand you have a new, supersecret procedure that's guaranteed to get results. I'll do anything, Doctor—I've *got* to lose sixty pounds, fast."

Fingertips together, the famous doctor reflected briefly, then asked Winfrey to undress completely. She obliged.

"Now get on all fours." She obeyed.

"Now move over there by the potted palm." Mystified but assuming this was all part of the program, Winfrey crawled over.

"Hmmmm." The doctor studied her closely. "Come this way a bit, next to that filing cabinet. . . . good, stop."

"Dr. Borgman, can you please explain what you're doing?" asked Winfrey at last, looking up plaintively. "Is this really going to help me lose weight fast?"

"Of course not," answered the doctor. "I'm just trying to figure out where to put the new leather couch I ordered."

•

What happened when Dolly Parton dropped a Walkman down her shirt?

The hills came to life with the sound of music.

Did you hear Harrison Ford was in a porno movie?
 It was called, "In Diana Jones."

Not long after David Dinkins was elected Mayor of New York, he was riding home with his wife in the limousine. And whom should they spot on a street corner but a man, none too prosperous looking, to whom Mrs. Dinkins had once been engaged.

 Dinkins turned to her and said smugly, "Now aren't you glad you married *me?*"

 "If I'd married *him,*" she responded tartly, *"he'd* be mayor."

What's brown and smells and wants to hold your hand?
 John Lennon.

Did you hear the sad news that the California Raisins are dead?

All the police know so far is that it was a cereal killer. . . .

•

What famous movie star comes to mind when you see a guy with a big beard smoking a big cigar?

Lassie, taking a shit.

•

The dentist was shocked when the gorgeous girl opened her mouth and revealed a row of smashed and broken front teeth. "Oh my goodness," he gasped. "What happened to you?"

"I'm not quite sure," she admitted, wincing. "I was going down on this reporter named Clark Kent, and the next thing I knew, his dick turned to iron."

•

Why's Nelson Mandela like an old WWII K-ration?

They've both spent a long, long time in the can.

•

What do the German Army and Elizabeth Taylor have in common?
They both lost the Battle of the Bulge.

•

Did you hear Billy Martin was on the radio?
And on the steering wheel, and on the dashboard . . .

•

What did Billy Martin do that no other ballplayer could?
Die sliding home.

•

How come he wanted to be cremated?
He wanted to get fired again.

•

What were Martin's last words?
"I said 'Bud light', not 'hard right!' "

Seen the new Dolly Parton doll?
  Plug it in and the tits swell up.

●

George Washington will go down in history for saying, "I cannot tell a lie."
  Richard Nixon will go down in history for saying, "I can't tell the truth."
  Ronald Reagan will go down in history for saying, "Uh . . . I forgot."

●

What do Madonna and a Boeing 747 have in common?
  They both have black boxes.

●

What looks like a dog and has wings?
  Linda McCartney.

●

You know Richard Gere had to go to the hospital . . .
. . . to have a mole removed.

•

Did you hear the new song for Covenant House?
"He's sixteen, he's homeless, and he's mine . . ."

•

Did you hear about the new, all-expenses-paid celebrity vacation for losers?

Christa McAuliffe flies you to Miami (unless you want to take the bus with Gloria Estefan), Rock Hudson sets you up on a date, Len Bias scores you some coke, you go barhopping with Willie Smith and Ted Kennedy, Lenny Dykstra drives you to a family picnic with the Brandos, Billy Idol rides you back on his motorcycle, and Rob Lowe will stay home and watch your kids!

OLD AGE

Millie Hawkes was pushing eighty-five, and her constipation finally became so acute that she made an appointment with an internist. "I've got it bad," she confessed. "My bowels haven't moved in over a week."

"I see," said the doctor, making a note on his chart. "And what do you do for it?"

"Well, I give it every opportunity, not that it seems to matter," she answered. "I sit in the bathroom for a good half an hour every morning, and almost that long after supper, too."

"That's not quite what I meant, Mrs. Hawkes," the doctor interrupted gently. "I mean, do you take anything?"

"Naturally," replied the old woman tartly. "I take a book."

●

Why is sex like insurance?
The older you get, the more it costs.

"What's wrong, sonny?" asked the old fellow sympathetically, coming over to a little kid who was sobbing his heart out on the curb.

The boy gulped, "I'm crying because I can't do the things that the big boys do."

So the old man sat down and wept too.

•

When Irving retired, he and his much younger wife moved to Boca Raton. Once they'd settled in, he decided it was about time to make up a will, so he made an appointment with a lawyer. "It's nice and straightforward," he instructed the attorney. "Everything goes to Rachel—the house, the car, the pension, the life insurance—on condition that she remarry within the year."

"Fine, Mr. Patron," said the lawyer. "But do you mind my asking why the condition?"

"Simple: I want at least one person to be sorry I died."

•

What was in the spinster's heart-shaped locket?
A picture of a candle.

•

The little old lady seated herself right behind the bus driver. Every ten minutes or so, she'd pipe up, "Have we reached Oriskany Falls, yet, sonny?"

"No, lady, not yet. I'll let you know," he replied, time after time. The hours passed, the old woman kept asking for Oriskany Falls, and finally the little town came into view. Sighing with relief, the driver slammed on the brakes, pulled over, and called out, "This is where you get out, lady."

"Is this Oriskany Falls?"

"YES!" he bellowed. "Get out!"

"Oh, I'm going all the way to Albany, sonny," she explained sweetly. "It's just that my daughter told me that when we got this far, I should take my blood pressure pill."

●

Why's an aging prostitute like a Timex watch?
  They both take a licking and keep on ticking.

●

What's the best thing about turning sixty-five?
  No more calls from insurance salesmen.

●

The two old women decided to vacation at a Catskills mountain resort. "Boy, the food at this place is really terrible," commented Gladys over dinner the first night.

Sylvia nodded in agreement. "Yeah, and such small portions."

•

The aged couple came into town for their annual physical. "You go in first, Paw," said the old woman, settling down to her knitting in the waiting room.

In a little while, the old codger stuck his head out of the doctor's office. "Maw," he called out, scratching his head, "do we have intercourse?"

"If I've told you once, I've told you a dozen times, Paw," she scolded, "we have Blue Cross and Blue Shield."

MISCELLANEOUS

As soon as they had finished making love, Susie jumped up from the bed and started packing her suitcase.

"What on Earth are you doing?" asked her puzzled husband.

"In Las Vegas I could get two hundred dollars for what I just gave you for free," she pointed out, "so I'm moving to Las Vegas."

This was enough to provoke her husband to jump up and begin packing *his* bags.

"What're you up to?" asked Susie in surprise.

"I'm following you to Las Vegas," he replied. "I've *got* to see you live off six hundred dollars a year."

•

How many doctors does it take to change a light bulb?
It depends on what kind of insurance the bulb has.

Little Freddy was playing airplane with a cardboard box in his back yard. "Vroom, vroom, rat-a-tat-a-tat," he yelled happily. "Here I am, a real U.S. Army pilot, flying at thirty thousand feet."

Little Louise looked over the fence and called, "Can I play, too?"

"Sure you can," called out the little boy, adjusting his goggles. "Lemme bring her in nice and slow like a real Army pilot and I'll take you up for a spin."

Louise climbed in behind him. "Fasten your seatbelt," ordered the boy, checking his imaginary gauges and roaring like a jet engine. "I'm a real Army pilot, so prepare for take-off." The little girl squealed in excitement as the plane roared through imaginary clouds and flawlessly performed imaginary barrel rolls. But as soon as they reached cruising altitude, she announced she had to pee.

"Can't scrub the mission," announced Freddy matter-of-factly. "This is the U. S. Army—you'll have to hold it, soldier." But in a few minutes he looked down and noticed a yellow stream trickling through the cockpit. Following it back, he observed with fascination its origin in little Louise's snatch. "Can I touch it?" he asked.

Louise nodded.

"Nice," he commented suavely.

"Would you like to kiss it?" she asked coyly.

"Gee," stammered Freddy, "I'm not a *real* Army pilot, you know."

The lawyer marched into the brig and announced that she had some good news and some bad news.

"What's the bad news?" asked the hulking private, who'd been found guilty of bludgeoning an inoffensive ensign to death.

"The provost marshal refuses to issue a stay of execution."

The prisoner paled and collapsed onto his bunk. "What's the good news?"

The lawyer flashed him an encouraging smile. "I got your voltage reduced."

•

Did you know that once you get married, you can look forward to three different kinds of sex?

—First there's House Sex, when you make love all over the house: on the floor, on the kitchen table, in the garage, anywhere, anytime.

—Then comes Bedroom Sex: once the kids are bathed and fed and asleep, the shades pulled, and the door locked, you make love in the bedroom.

—Last comes Hall Sex. That's when you pass each other in the hall and snarl, "Fuck you."

•

"Don't let me pressure you, Mrs. Schmidt," said the aggressive life-insurance salesman. "Why don't you sleep on my offer and call me in the morning? If you wake up."

•

Following Thomson's physical, Dr. Munro sent his patient a bill. When a month went by without a remittance, Munro sent another bill, and then another, and then another, but to no avail. Finally, he sent Thomson a pathetic letter, claiming desperately straitened circumstances and enclosing a picture of his infant daughter. On the back of the snapshot, he wrote, "The reason I need the money you owe me."

Barely a week later a response from Thomson arrived in the mail. Munro ripped it open eagerly, and found himself holding a picture of a gorgeous woman in a mink coat. On the back of the photograph, his patient had scrawled, "The reason I can't pay."

•

"Mom, hey, Mom! Lennie passed his bar exam so we're going to get married next week!" The bride-to-be was ecstatic.

"Gee, honey, don't you think you two should wait till he's been practicing for a year or so?" cautioned her mother.

"Oh Mom," said the bride with a blush, "we've *been* practicing."

When Mr. Fine was audited, the IRS took exception to certain deductions, among them one for the birth of a child. "She was born in January," the auditor explained.

"So?" Fine protested. "It was last year's business."

•

Clark telephoned the police and informed the desk sergeant that he'd been getting threatening letters. "Isn't that against the law?" he blustered.

"It certainly is," replied the desk sergeant. "Have you any idea who the sender is?"

"Yeah," Clark admitted, "my girlfriend's husband."

•

"So tell me, Ms. Harris," asked the personnel director, "have you any other skills you think might be worth mentioning?"

"Actually, yes," said the applicant modestly. "Last year I had two short stories published in national magazines, and finished a novel."

"Very impressive," commented the interviewer. "But I was thinking of skills you could apply during office hours."

The applicant explained brightly, "Oh, that was during office hours."

How do you use a condom twice?

Turn it inside out and shake the fuck out of it.

•

"My daughter Lauren thinks money grows on trees," the overworked businessman complained to his secretary one day. "Tonight she's getting a talking-to that'll really get across the value of a dollar."

"How'd it go?" asked the secretary the next morning.

"Not so good," he admitted glumly. "Now the kid wants her allowance in Deutschmarks."

•

Have you seen the new home surgery kit available via mail order?

It's called Suture Self.

•

The death of a pillar of the community whose morning coffee had been laced with arsenic by his wife of thirty years was the talk of the town for months. Eckhardt, the defense attorney, knew he had his work cut out, and was trying to make his not-very-appealing client appear more sympathetic to the jury. "Tell me, Mrs. Ross, was there any point during the commission of the crime at which you felt pity for your husband?" he asked. Eckhardt was delighted when the woman nodded and said she had.

"And when was that?" the lawyer inquired delicately.

"When he asked for a second cup."

•

Swensen grew up on a remote dairy farm in Minnesota, and finally decided it was time to get some experience with women. So he drove the pick-up into the nearest city and managed to find a prostitute who was more than willing to initiate him into the mysteries of sex.

Undressing, the hooker lay down and proceeded to instruct him carefully. "Stick it in, honey . . . all the way . . . now pull it out . . . okay, back in, slowly . . . more, oooh, more. . . . Now back out again—"

"For Christ's sake," interrupted the sweating farm boy, "could you make up your mind?"

•

At the monthly staff meeting, the hospital director brought up the head nurse's accusation that Dr. Stone had addressed her in a rude and vulgar manner. "We must censure this sort of behavior," the chief pointed out. "Have you anything to say in your defense?"

"Let me explain the extenuating circumstances," requested Dr. Stone. "First of all, my alarm didn't go off. So when I saw how late I was I jumped out of bed, caught my foot in the sheets and fell over, smacking my head into the bedside table and breaking the lamp. As I was shaving the doorbell rang, and I cut myself. It was a young fellow selling encyclopedias, and I had to buy *A* through *G* before I could get rid of him. I'd forgotten my bagel in the toaster oven, so it was burnt and my coffee was cold. On my way to the car I slipped, bruising my knee and tearing my coat, and then the battery turned out to be dead. It took forty-five minutes for the serviceman to come over and get the car started, which cost me eighty-five dollars. I should have taken a cab anyway, because in the hospital parking lot the snowplow ran into the car, totalling the front end."

Dr. Stone took a deep breath and continued. "And when I finally got to my office and sat down at my desk to collect myself, Nurse McMahon burst in and said, 'Doctor, that shipment of six dozen thermometers just arrived—where do you want me to put them?' "

•

The nouveau-riche real-estate developer splurged on a Rolls-Royce Silver Shadow and couldn't wait to show it off. So after a meeting with the bank, he offered one of the senior bank officers a ride home. "Whaddaya think?" he couldn't resist asking his passenger after a mile or two. "Pretty classy, eh? I bet you've never ridden in one of these before."

"Actually I have," replied the banker graciously, "but this is my first time in the front seat."

•

The slave driver of the Roman galleon leered down at his galley slaves and bellowed, "I've got some good news and some bad news. The good news is that you'll be getting double rations tonight."

The murmuring of the surprised slaves was interrupted by the bellow of the slave driver. "The bad news is that the commander's son wants to water-ski."

•

Miss Horn was grotesquely overweight, so her doctor finally prescribed a strict regimen, telling her it was the only way to avoid serious health problems in the future. "I want you to eat normally for two days, but then skip a day, drinking only water. Repeat this three times, and by the time I see you next Thursday you'll have lost at least six pounds."

The patient promised to obey, and indeed when she showed up for the appointment she was almost fifteen pounds lighter.

"Excellent progress, Miss Horn," enthused the doctor, quite amazed. "And you lost all this weight simply by following my instructions?"

Miss Horn nodded. "It wasn't easy, though, Doctor,"

she admitted. "On that third day, I felt like I was about to die."

"From hunger, eh?" The doctor clucked sympathetically.

"No, no," she explained, "from skipping."

•

A man walked into a fancy dress store and announced to the owner, "I'm the greatest salesperson ever. And I want a job."

"That's quite a claim," the owner responded, "but unfortunately I don't have any openings."

Undaunted the salesperson asked, "How many dresses does your best employee sell in a day?"

"Five or six," the owner answered.

Without blinking an eye, the fellow claimed, "I'll sell twelve and I'll do it without pay or commission."

The owner, knowing she couldn't lose, agreed. And, indeed, just an hour before closing, the new salesperson had sold eighteen dresses. "Do I get the job now?" he asked.

"I've got one more test for you," the owner declared. She went back to the storeroom and then came out with the most hideous dress imaginable. "Sell this dress by the time the store closes tonight and you've got a job."

Forty-five minutes later, the guy marched into her office and threw down the sales receipt. "I'm impressed," the owner admitted in amazement. "You've got the job. How on Earth did you convince somebody to buy that thing?"

"Getting the woman to buy it wasn't a problem. The hard part was strangling her seeing-eye dog."

•

During basic training, the new recruits were policing the grounds in front of the barracks when a platoon of WACs came by. The privates straightened up and looked the women over hungrily, and the WACs couldn't resist getting an eyeful themselves.

That was enough for their drill sergeant. Ordering the women into formation facing the barracks, she instructed the red-faced platoon to take a good look. "There are six hundred miles of dick on this base," she bellowed, "and let me make one thing perfectly clear: you girls aren't getting an inch of it."

•

A fellow applying for a job as a flagman with the Baltimore & Ohio Railroad was told the job was his if he could correctly answer a single question: as flagman, what would he do if he saw the Continental Express coming from the east at 100 mph and the Century Limited heading west at 90 mph on the same track?

The applicant pondered for a moment, then answered, "I'd fetch my brother-in-law."

"What good would that do?" asked the interviewer. "Has he worked on the railroad?"

"Nope—he ain't never seen a train accident."

Ike left work early one day, and when he opened the front door he found his wife on all fours scrubbing the hall rug. She wasn't wearing anything but her underwear, so Ike snuck up behind her, pulled down her panties, and screwed her doggie-style right then and there. And then he smacked her in the head.

"Ike!" she yelped. "After such a nice surprise, why'd you go and do something so nasty to me?"

"Because, Irene," he replied gruffly, "you never looked to see who it was."

•

What do you call a pretty girl on an Aggie campus?
   A visitor.

•

After the plane reached cruising altitude, the captain's voice came over the intercom with the usual information about the speed and altitude, weather conditions and the estimated arrival time. Then, not realizing the microphone was still on, the pilot was heard to say to the co-pilot, "You take over. I'm gonna take a dump and then screw that cute new stewardess."

Of course everyone on the plane overheard this indiscreet announcement, and the nearest stewardess abandoned her beverage cart to dash up to the cockpit and shut off the mike before more damage could be done.

"No need to rush, dearie," said an old woman, grabbing the stewardess's elbow as she flew past. "He said he had to go to the bathroom first, remember?"

•

What's organic dental floss?
Pubic hair.

•

A drunk walked into a bar sobbing as though his heart were broken. "Hey buddy, what's wrong?" asked one of the men hanging out at the bar.

"I did a horrible thing," confessed the drunk, burying his head in his arms. "Just a couple of hours ago, I sold my wife to someone for a bottle of vodka."

"Jeez, no wonder you feel bad," sympathized his companion. "That *was* a horrible thing to do. And now I guess you want her back, huh?"

"I sure do," moaned the drunk.

"I guess you realized you shouldn't have sold her because you really loved her, huh?"

"Oh, no, that's not it," he replied, sobbing louder than ever. "I want her back because I'm thirsty again."

•

"How'd you get along with your new daddy while I was on my business trip?" asked the recently-remarried woman.

"Fine, Mommy," responded her eight-year-old. "Every morning he took me out on the lake in a rowboat and let me swim back to shore."

"Gee, honey, wasn't that kind of a long swim?"

"Not too bad. The tough part was getting out of the bag first."

•

What's the fastest way to make a million dollars?

Become a plastic surgeon and work part-time.

•

"Listen, tomorrow night the Giants are playing Chicago," said Tom, leaning over his buddy's desk. "You're going to be there, aren't you? It's a big game."

"Nah," said Matt with a shrug. "You know my wife won't let me go."

"You jerk, don't you know how to handle her?" asked Tom. When Matt shook his head glumly, Tom explained with a smirk, "Well, an hour or so before the game you simply grab her, drag her upstairs, tear off her clothes and fuck her silly. Then you stand up and announce, 'I'm off to the ball game,' and out you go."

On Monday morning Tom made a beeline for Matt's

office. "Well?" he demanded. "I didn't see you at the stadium—what happened?"

"I'll tell you," said Matt. "Like you said, an hour or so before game time, I grabbed Patty, carried her upstairs, and threw her onto the bed . . ."

"Yeah, and then what?" pursued his buddy.

"And then just as I got her panties off and was unzipping my fly, I thought to myself, what the hell, the Giants haven't been playing that well lately."

•

What do you call one pervert too many?

An extrovert.

•

The homeowner got into his grubbiest clothes one Saturday morning and set about all the chores he'd been putting off for weeks. He'd cleaned out the garage, pruned the hedge, and was halfway through mowing the lawn when a guy pulled up in front of the house in a fancy sports car and called out, "Say, buddy, what do you get for that yard work?"

The fellow thought for a minute, then yelled back, "The lady who lives here lets me sleep with her."

TOO TASTELESS TO BE
INCLUDED

Have you heard about Tempura House?

It's the new halfway house for lightly battered women.

•

What's the definition of a virgin El Salvador soldier?

One who hasn't raped a nun yet.

•

The buck private served under a sadistic sergeant, who gave him latrine duty so many days in a row that he decided he had to get out of the Army on a Section Eight. The next day found him with latrine duty once again. He scrubbed until the whole room was hospital-clean, then took a big gob of peanut butter and stuck it on the last toilet seat.

"What's that?" growled the sergeant, delighted to have found something to get on the soldier's case about. "Looks like shit, doesn't it, asswipe?"

The private came over, scooped up some of the stuff on his finger, and popped it right in his mouth. "Well, sir," he reported thoughtfully, "it sure ain't piss."

•

What goes "hop, skip, jump, ka-blam!"?
Nicaraguan children playing in a mine field.

Would you like to see your favorite tasteless jokes in print? If so, send them to:

Blanche Knott
c/o St. Martin's Press
175 Fifth Avenue
New York, N.Y. 10010

I'm sorry, but no compensation or credit can be given. But I *love* hearing from my tasteless readers.